Do Something Today Your Future Self Will Thank You For: Inspirational Journal
Motivational Green Lined Notebook
Paperback ISBN: 978-1-989733-16-5